THE NATURE LIBRARY

DOGS

YVONNE REES

CRESCENT BOOKS
NEW YORK

This 1991 edition published by Crescent Books,
distributed by Outlet Book Company, Inc,
a Random House Company, 225 Park Avenue South,
New York, New York 10003.

Printed and bound in Hong Kong

ISBN 0-517-05152-4

8 7 6 5 4 3 2 1

Library of Congress Cataloging-in-Publication Data
Dogs
   p. cm – (Nature Library)
  Includes index.
  Summary: Explores the world of dogs, discussing their care, training,
different breeds, and other aspects.
  ISBN 0-517-05152-4 : $6.99
  1. Dogs – Juvenile literature.   (1. Dogs.)   I. Series.
SF426.5 D62 1991   90-41200
636.7 – dc20   CIP
                                                             AC

Credits
Edited and designed: Ideas into Print, Vera Rogers and Stuart Watkinson
Layouts: Stonecastle Graphics Ltd. **Editorial assistance:** Joanne King
Picture Editors: Annette Lerner, John Kaprielian
Photographs: Photo Researchers Inc. New York, and Marc Henrie
Commissioning Editor: Andrew Preston
Production: Ruth Arthur, Sally Connolly, David Proffit, Andrew Whitelaw
Director of Production: Gerald Hughes
Director of Publishing: David Gibbon
Typesetting: SX Composing Ltd.
Color separations: Scantrans Pte. Ltd., Singapore

The Author

Yvonne Rees is a writer and lecturer on a wide range of subjects, including
wildlife and animals. She shares her home in the country with a variety of
domestic animals (and many wild ones), including two cats and two dogs.
Looking after pets for friends and neighbors has involved Yvonne in
keeping an eye on anything from quails and peacocks to cats, dogs, goats,
hens and sheep. In her spare time she likes to paint, and has often turned
her hand to preparing pet portraits for proud owners.

CONTENTS

Above: Three Scottish Terriers pose proudly for the camera. These are sporty little terriers, renowned for being intensely loyal to their owners and standing their ground if threatened. They love the outdoor life and thrive on exercise.

Left: A Beagle puppy, with all the natural charm of an inquiring youngster. These affectionate dogs are superb with children and will happily live alongside other pets in the house. Do remember that they are hounds and have a tendency to wander given the chance.

ANCESTORS OF THE DOMESTIC DOG

All dogs are thought to be descended from early mammals called miacids that lived more than 50 million years ago. These early forms of dog existed in many sizes and shapes, from a very small ferret-type creature, to something closely resembling our present-day wolf, and displayed the same tooth structure as modern domesticated and wild dogs.

Dogs have been classed as Carnivora, an order that includes such differing species as the hyena and the marten, as well as the Canidae family of dogs, wolves, jackals and wild dogs. The first members of the Canidae originated around 25 million years ago in North America and eventually spread westwards across the Bering Strait (then land). Some went south towards South America and evolved into foxes.

We do not know when man first started to trap wolves – considered the most likely antecedent to our domestic dog – and to breed them in captivity, but the evidence of the most ancient cave paintings suggests that it must have been very early in his own development. Packs of wolves will naturally follow and hang around human settlements, both nomadic and permanent, in the hope of scavenging food, so it seems highly likely that man started to feed the cubs, and eventually restrained them as they became tamer. By the Bronze Age (about 3,500-1,000 B.C.), they were certainly being used to help with hunting and guarding flocks. By this time, too, the tamed dog had started to develop into five groups, from which all today's breeds have evolved: the spitz type, sheepdogs, mastiffs, pointers and greyhounds. Later, when man began to travel as soldier, explorer, settler and merchant trader, cross-breeding occurred between dogs all over the world.

Left: Wolves share many instincts and characteristics with the dog we know today, and it is highly likely that the earliest breeds developed from local wolf packs that kept close to human encampments. However, there is evidence that by 12,000 B.C., man's hunting companion was quite definitely doglike and not wolflike in appearance.

Left: The Australian wild dog, or Dingo, is believed to be very like the earliest domesticated dog to look at, although the wolf is closer in its habits and behaviour.

Below: Like dogs, wolves are highly adaptable to their surroundings, and were once found in all parts of the world, which may explain the great variety of different domestic dog breeds. This is the maned wolf, *Chrysocyon brachyurus*, whose antecedents go back some 300,000 years.

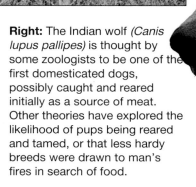

Left: Although it seems a likely candidate as one of the dog's earliest ancestors, the easily tamed jackal has now been largely ruled out on the grounds that it has not been found to mix or communicate with dogs.

Above: A marked physical resemblance to the wolf has led to the belief that the German Shepherd dog is directly related to wolves, although there is no firm evidence for this. It is sometimes called the Alsatian Wolf Dog.

Right: The Indian wolf *(Canis lupus pallipes)* is thought by some zoologists to be one of the first domesticated dogs, possibly caught and reared initially as a source of meat. Other theories have explored the likelihood of pups being reared and tamed, or that less hardy breeds were drawn to man's fires in search of food.

DOGS IN ANCIENT TIMES

Dogs feature in man's earliest carvings, statues and paintings, giving plenty of clues to the appearance of the breeds and the role they played in human society. The mastiff and greyhound types seem to have been the most popular, probably because their strength, speed, grace or intelligence made them especially suited to hunting and guard duties or inspired man to worship them.

Several ancient cultures worshipped dog-headed gods: in Ancient Japan, it was believed that anyone committing suicide in the name of their dog-headed deity would be promised eternal joy in the afterlife. The Egyptian dog-headed or wolf-headed god, Anubis, was the god of the dead and was believed to guide human souls to eternity. The Egyptians also worshipped a greyhound-type of creature in the form of the god of evil, Seth, depicted with long pointed ears and a long wispy tail. The Pharaohs who ruled

Ancient Egypt also used a long-legged, fast-running type of dog for hunting. Famous in Greek mythology is Cerberus, a three-headed dog with a dragon's tail that guarded the entrance to the Underworld. The Greeks used mastiffs as guard dogs and hounds for hunting. The Romans preferred bloodhounds and greyhounds for hunting, plus a smaller breed, which they developed for tracking small game. This eventually became our modern pointer. The Romans used mastiffs as guard dogs and for sport: the dogs would be put to fight in an arena. The passion for hunting in the Middle Ages encouraged cross-breeding and the development of specific breeds, such as terriers and greyhounds, to hunt hare, deer and game birds. Mastiffs were used to bring down larger game. These categories were expanded and refined during the sixteenth century, and contemporary paintings are a good indication of the range of breeds and purpose – from hunting to a lady's lap dog.

Above: You can frequently identify dogs as pets or guards on ancient pictures and pottery. This beautiful, highly decorated amphora is believed to date from about the year 540 B.C.

Left: Dogs were used as trained aggressors and man's close companion from earliest times. These large, well-muscled Assyrian war dogs have been depicted on the walls of the Palace of Ashurbanipal.

Left: Pet dogs are often shown with their owners in portraits. This elegant lady, painted in about 1685 by William Wissing, obviously wanted to be immortalized with her stylish Italian Greyhound.

Above: Until relatively recently, the more ferocious dog breeds provided popular sport. Natural fighters, such as this Pit Bull Terrier, may still be used for that purpose, although such practices are now discouraged.

Right: A noble, but mythological, dog heraldically displayed in stone at Kew Gardens in the UK.

Below: In the sixth century, Phoenician traders were probably responsible for the popularity of mastiffs as war dogs in Europe. The Romans also liked to pit these aggressive dogs against bears, bulls and lions for sporting purposes.

THE ANATOMY OF A DOG

Today's dogs span a great variety of shapes and sizes, from the Great Dane, as big as a small pony, to miniature breeds, such as the Papillon, a member of the toy spaniel family, small enough to fit into a pocket or lady's handbag.

All dogs have certain characteristics in common, such as the basic skeleton, body functions and a highly efficient sense of smell and hearing. However, they have all developed special skills and refinements, either as the result of a deliberate breeding policy or in order to adapt to their environment. For example, the Husky and Saint Bernard have thicker skin and a double coat to cope with sub-zero temperatures. Dogs even have very different kinds of tails, from the aerodynamic tail of the greyhound to the pug's tight coil or the feathery extravagance of an English Setter. The tails are designed to serve a practical purpose, as well as a decorative one – they play a vital part in the manoeuvrability of the animal, especially where the dog is built for speed or hunting. Watch a Greyhound or a Whippet competing on the race circuit or a Saluki in the heat of a chase and notice how the tail is used to counterbalance the animal's weight as it turns corners.

Coat type also has its function – it might be curly and rich in oils, making the dog an ideal sporting breed for land and water, or short and sleek as suede, the coat of a good fighter. The Poodle's coat grows all the time and needs regular clipping, but the Mexican Hairless hardly has a coat at all. Coat colours and markings are even more varied; some breeds, such as terriers, offer a particularly wide range of types.

Above: Distinguishable by its rough shaggy coat, the Briard is, in fact, an agile and muscular animal under all that hair. Its coat is an important asset when it is working as an active sheepdog in France.

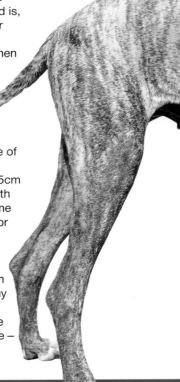

Right: The Great Dane is one of the largest dog breeds in the world, standing at least 71-75cm (28-30in) high as an adult, with an arched belly and handsome head. It was originally bred for hunting wild boar.

Left: Originally a large gundog, poodles now come in various sizes, including the tiny Toy Poodle, an extremely popular lap dog. However, the basic shape remains the same – high-tailed and muscular.

Right: Solid and stocky, with a thrusting flattened head and deep set eyes, the Bull Terrier is clearly a born fighter and aggressor.

Above: The intelligent-looking Canaan from Israel is not yet recognized as an authorized breed, but has the erect pointed ears and almost wolflike profile of the German Shepherd Dog.

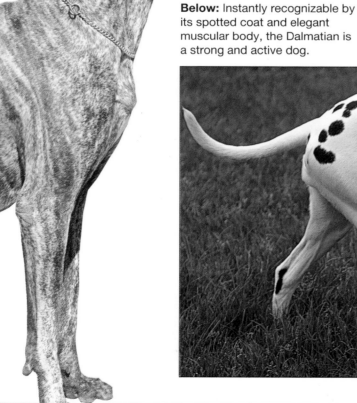

Below: Instantly recognizable by its spotted coat and elegant muscular body, the Dalmatian is a strong and active dog.

Above: The Basset Hound's soulful profile, with large floppy ears and sad eyes, hides a vigorous, but friendly nature.

Above: A thick mane of hair makes the friendly Chow Chow resemble a cuddly teddy bear. It belongs to the Spitz family.

A DOG FOR YOU

The first thing to consider when buying a dog, or even accepting one as a gift, is whether you can give it the kind of life and provide the conditions it needs. Your choice of dog will also be affected by what you hope for from your dog: a companionable pet in a small city apartment; a sporting gundog; a friend for the family or an efficient guard dog. Differences in size, temperament and certain specialist skills, such as retrieving or a quick and ready intelligence, make certain breeds better suited to a particular role and lifestyle than others. It is only fair to the dog to choose wisely. Although owning a dog can be great fun, it is a hard life for the animal if you do not have the time to exercise it, cannot afford to feed it properly or if you

have to leave a large, boisterous dog shut up indoors for long periods. Unlike caged birds or tropical fish, which take very little time to feed and clean, or cats, which are naturally far more independent creatures, dogs need plenty of attention, and cannot be allowed to roam freely in town or countryside.

Having accepted the responsibility of care, you must carefully consider which type of dog you would like. If you are looking for an enjoyable pet of no pedigree, a trip to your local dog's home will find plenty of irresistible mongrels. Their appearance will provide clues to the breed of their parents and this in turn will give you some idea of the dog's requirements and temperament. If there are young children in the house, choose a puppy of a good-natured breed, so that they can grow up and be taught together. On the other hand, an elderly person would be well advised to choose a more mature animal that has already been trained and does not need a great deal of exercise.

If you fancy a particular pedigree breed or are interested in breeding dogs, you should only buy from an accredited dealer, checking the relevant certificates carefully. Any dog you buy must be in good condition, happy and obviously well looked after.

Above: Choosing a puppy can be difficult – they all look so appealing. Do have some idea of the type of dog you want before you go to the kennels or you may lose your heart to an unsuitable breed.

Above: The docile and affectionate Saint Bernard is an excellent choice if you are looking for a large, family dog.

Left: Given loving care and sufficient attention, a strong relationship will develop between a dog and its owner, resulting in a lasting trust on each side, especially if begun as a puppy.

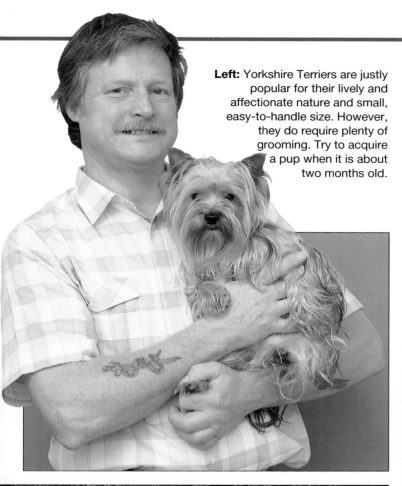

Left: Yorkshire Terriers are justly popular for their lively and affectionate nature and small, easy-to-handle size. However, they do require plenty of grooming. Try to acquire a pup when it is about two months old.

Above: As well as being a superb guard dog, the German Shepherd Dog also makes a fine pet and loyal companion. Begin its training while it is still young, in order to ensure complete obedience and respect.

Above: If you enjoy taking plenty of fresh air and exercise, a big active dog, such as this Dobermann, can make an ideal companion, as well as an excellent guard dog.

Right: Puppies and children are ideal companions. By playing and growing up with a dog, children soon learn to become responsible for their pets and to value the trust placed in them.

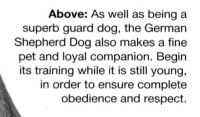

COPING WITH A NEW PUPPY

A new puppy in the household can be great fun, but a lot of hard work. You will need to devote a good deal of care and attention to your new puppy, although this varies according to the breed and age of the animal. A single pup tends to become easily bored and will quickly get into mischief. Never leave anything you value in the same room as a puppy, as it will chew absolutely everything, from your best furniture and favourite shoes to the bottom of the door.

When newly weaned from their mother and introduced into a strange home, some pups will yap constantly and even go off their food for a while, but do not become overly concerned; patience and time will resolve these problems. Night times are usually the hardest for a young puppy; it will feel lonely and neglected, so try providing a couple of toys and a familiar sack or blanket for reassurance. Regular feeding and the right amount of food are also important. 'Little and often' is usually recommended and should provide a well-balanced diet, especially while the puppy is growing.

It is important for children to be taught that a young pup is not a toy or bean bag to be bashed or dragged around. They may unintentionally hurt the dog and, should the animal lose patience, it might turn on the children, hurting them in the process. If there is already a dog in the house, it may befriend a new puppy immediately, but usually it will not like the idea of this potential threat to its dominance and security and may treat the newcomer quite badly. Again, time and patience spent in introducing the animals to one another will probably solve the problem. Be prepared to spend at least a few hours a day in the company of any new puppy, learning its habits and developing character and teaching it the essentials of home life; most breeds are quick and willing learners. Patience will soon convert a nuisance into a pleasure.

Right: Puppies should be handled from about six to eight weeks old or they will never become used to human contact. Learn to pick up and hold the animal correctly, so that it feels safe and properly supported in your arms.

Below: The mother dog will take good care of her pups and will even, on occasion, suckle whelps from another litter.

Above: Exercise and play are very important to a puppy's physical and mental development. They allow the dog to test its vital senses of smell, sight and taste, as well as the chance to stretch its muscles.

Above: Do not forget that the cuddliest, most endearing puppies may grow into large dogs, requiring plenty of space and vigorous exercise. This Saint Bernard will make a good family dog, nevertheless.

Left: Toilet training is a lengthy process and requires great patience from the owner. Teach your pet to restrict itself to one area from the earliest age and start taking it outside six times a day from three months old.

Above: Yelping, howling and barking are natural to the young dog, and an essential element during play to develop natural instincts — although it may not always be to the owner's liking!

Left: Puppies should be weaned from the end of their fourth week. Initially, you can offer the pups the same food as their mother four times a day, and add a few extra vitamins, depending on how well the youngsters seem to be growing.

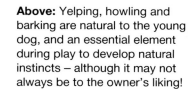

FEEDING YOUR DOG

It is most important to feed your dog sensibly. Poor diet will soon cause it to become listless, with a dull coat and, possibly, prone to infection. Inadequate feeding may be due to laziness or meanness on the part of the owner. Table scraps are not good enough, nor are biscuits alone, unless they are part of a dry mix, recommended as a completely balanced feed. Various convenient and ready-to-use dog foods are available. Complete dried meals can be bought by the sack and are easily reconstituted with water or they may be designed as a crunchy supplement, to be added to tinned or fresh meats. Canned meat is more expensive but, again, usually provides a balance of proteins, vitamins and minerals.

The least expensive, but obviously more time consuming option, is to mix up a balanced feed yourself. It will be your responsibility to ensure that the feed includes the right proportions of meat or offal; carbohydrate, such as broken rice, meal, corn, bread or biscuits; cooked vegetables; fats – sunflower or corn oil are best, and an appropriate vitamin or mineral supplement. Always clean out half-eaten bowls of food and never top them up with fresh supplies; the old food will go stale and harbour germs. A fresh supply of water should also be available at all times.

Adult dogs are usually fed twice a day, and young puppies more frequently, until they are completely weaned. Dogs should be fed at regular times every day. If they know when to expect their food, it will prevent them fretting. It is not a good idea to feed between meals, except as a reward, and then the snippets should be kept to a minimum. If you keep more than one dog, provide separate bowls to prevent scuffles, especially if one dog is larger than the others.

Below: Feed your dog regular meals, preferably from the same dish and at roughly the same time every day. The amount of food should be regulated according to the dog's size and whether it is a pampered pet receiving little exercise or a highly active working dog.

Below: Most proprietary foods contain the correct balance of nutrients. However, if you prefer to make up your own mixture, you must ensure it includes all the necessary elements for health and vitality. This obviously takes a lot more time and effort.

Left: Some dogs will get up to all kinds of irresistible tricks to beg titbits from their owner's table. Do not encourage this habit, because in the long term it can cause problems, not only because the dog may become obese, but also if it starts to make a nuisance of itself.

Above: Young pups will happily eat out of the same dish. Later on, however, they should be given separate bowls to prevent them from squabbling. This will also help to ensure that one animal does not have a chance to dominate the other and get more than its fair share of food.

Above: Water should be available at all times: a big thirsty dog may otherwise resort to extreme measures.

Right: A well-fed dog will look bright-eyed and lively, be full of vigour and more resistant to disease – a dog to be proud of.

GROOMING YOUR DOG

To keep your dog trim and looking in good condition, you will need to maintain its coat in a clean, untangled state, whatever the breed. Smooth-haired dogs are obviously much easier to groom; because they do not attract so much dirt and debris, their coat is unlikely to become matted and there is less problem of moulting. Acquiring a long-haired breed of dog could be a mistake if you do not have the time to groom it thoroughly and regularly.

Regular grooming need not be too much of a chore, if you do not allow the coat to become matted. It not only keeps the coat clean, but also stimulates the skin and muscles. Dogs that are shedding their hair need extra grooming, especially if they are kept indoors. It will help to encourage new growth, and reduces the moulting time. If your dog happens to be a Poodle or Bedlington Terrier, you may need expert advice on grooming it correctly. Various scissors and clippers are available for trimming, but many owners prefer to take their pet to a salon for a regular clip and shampoo.

Dogs kept outdoors do not need to be groomed as often, or as thoroughly, because they become more hardy and need to maintain the natural oils in the hair. Dogs with extra dry or scaly skin can be given cod liver

Above: Wire-haired dogs are stripped between two and four times a year, using a special stripping knife that keeps the coat in trim. Regular brushing maintains the coat in good condition in the meantime.

oil, or a similar supplement, to improve its condition. When bathing or shampooing your dog, be careful not to get any water in the eyes or ears. Thoroughly rinse out the shampoo, as any left to dry on the skin may cause dryness and itching. A large dog that dislikes being given a bath can sometimes be difficult to handle, so try to get someone to help you.

Left: Long-haired breeds, such as this Swiss Mountain Dog, may need to be raked, combed and regularly bathed and brushed to remove dirt and matted hair. This prevents the coat becoming knotted and dull.

Above: Yorkshire Terriers should be brushed all over with a soft bristle brush. Trim the hair on the belly and paws before bathing and carefully drying the dog. After the bath, give the animal a good comb through.

Left: Encourage children to undertake every aspect of their pet's care, including grooming. Standing smaller dogs on a low stool or table makes them easier to reach and handle, but make sure they are secure.

Above: A grooming parlour or salon will give your dog a professional trim. This keeps certain breeds looking smart, and also makes them easier to groom between visits. Salons offer a range of treatments.

Below: A tin bath, large barrel or bowl is useful for washing dogs. You can use a hosepipe, but being able to immerse the dog completely in the water means you can give it a thorough scrub. Some dogs really enjoy bath sessions, especially if the water is warm.

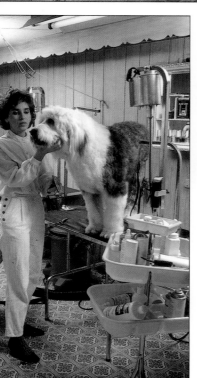

Above: Comb Yorkshire Terriers in a downward direction, from the middle of the back, and working from head to tail.

Left: Grooming a large dog, such as an Old English Sheepdog, may appear to be a daunting prospect. Good salons are equipped with the grooming tools and accessories needed to cope with a variety of breeds.

EXERCISE AND PLAY

Below: Dogs from the same litter or animals that have grown up together will enjoy a great many boisterous games.

All dogs, no matter what the breed, need some form of daily exercise. Obviously, smaller animals do not need as much room to run about in and should be able to get enough physical activity within the home or backyard. However, all dogs enjoy the stimulus of new scents and surroundings, and should be given the opportunity to go out as often as possible. A dog needs regular exercise in order to maintain suppleness of the muscles and joints, and to prevent it from putting on too much weight. A dog in bad shape should not be worked too hard initially, as this puts an enormous strain on the heart and can cause a fatal heart attack. Working dogs should be kept in trim once the season is over, so try to find some alternative form of work or play for them. Normally, a happy dog is one that spends the right amount of time either hunting or playing, and this can be reflected in the animal's personality. An under-exercised dog can become irritable and generally hard to cope with.

If you have a large garden or plenty of room adjoining your home, you may consider installing a dog-flap. This will help prevent fouling in the house, particularly during your absence, and allows your dog access to fresh air whenever required. It may cause problems on a wet day, if the dog is constantly running in and out with wet feet, so it is a good idea to

confine it to a single room. Alternatively, you could build a run or cage, allowing enough room for the dog to be able to move about freely and incorporating somewhere warm and dry for it to sleep.

Below: This Husky loves the water and will plunge into the coldest river. Other dogs are so reluctant, you have to throw them in to get their paws wet.

Below: Allowing your dog off the lead when out for exercise gives it a chance to have a really good run.

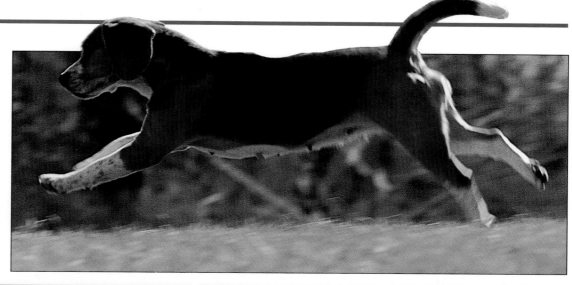

Right: Sprinting at full speed is an enjoyable experience for this Beagle, and provides good exercise for lungs, muscles and sinews. A dog travels at roughly four standard speeds: short strides, long strides, a brisk trot and full gallop.

Below: Keep your dog on a leash, particularly if it tends to be rather difficult to restrain. This will prevent the dog worrying sheep in the countryside, and other pets or pedestrians in urban areas.

Above: Dogs that are kept as part of the family will enjoy being taken for exercise in the context of a regular family outing.

Below: A wide range of 'fetch-and-carry' toys can be found in pet shops. They provide fun and exercise for every size of dog.

TRAINING YOUR DOG

Patience, time and plenty of encouragement are the three essential elements when training a dog. If you are not familiar with the animal, spend some time with it first and get to know it better, otherwise, it will not understand you and will tend to shy away when you give it commands. Sometimes a dog can be really stubborn and difficult to train – certain breeds are more headstrong than others. These dogs will need more intensive training before they learn to obey their master. Never shout at, or vent your temper on, a dog that does not deserve to be reprimanded; it will not understand why it is being reprimanded and will become nervous. When your dog has achieved a particular set goal, stroke it and reward it with lots of affection and kind words, such as: 'good dog' or 'well done'. Repeat this procedure each time it does something correctly. When the dog does something wrong, you must be quick to let it know by using a sudden sharper tone of voice. If the dog is on a lead, give it a firm tug. Say 'no' clearly and loudly.

Only someone who has had considerable previous experience should attempt to train more than one dog at the same time. You may be frustrated to find that unsuccessful training results in two dogs that are actually worse behaved than they were before. Some dogs will obey their handler, but act aggressively towards other people. Unless they are being trained as guard dogs, this attitude should be punished, because

Right: Teaching your dog to fetch and carry is one of the most basic and enjoyable training skills. Sporting breeds are quick to learn.

it could result in someone getting bitten. Sometimes you may need to use a muzzle, until you are satisfied that the dog can be trusted without it.

Whether you are training a dog to obey simple commands or for some more specific purpose, never let your animal think that it can do as it pleases. If this is the case, it will soon learn to become disobedient and become totally beyond any control.

Left: At special obedience classes, which are often held at your local park, your dog will learn more advanced skills, such as leaping over high obstacles.

Above: Some dogs can be trained for very special and important purposes, such as acting as a reliable guide and companion to a blind person.

Left: Teaching obedience is vital if the owner-dog relationship is to be successful and happy.

Below: This nine-week-old Springer pup is being taught to retrieve a sock, thus developing its natural skills early in life.

Left: Training an animal to become a professional guard dog is a long and rigorous process. It must learn to be fierce and aggressive, yet remain totally obedient.

Left: Most dogs will eagerly join in the fun of training, learning all kinds of amusing tricks, such as sitting up and begging, walking on their hind legs and even performing somersaults.

Right: The best way to train a dog is to attend special group sessions, where professional instructors teach you and your dog simple training and ring work.

SHOWING YOUR DOG

A first-prize rosette will make any dog owner proud, whether won at a big international show or local fete. It is official recognition that your dog is in excellent condition, has a lively, interesting character or is a fine example of its breed.

Showing your dog can be expensive – it will cost more than you could ever hope to collect in prize money, unless the dog is a first-class champion. However, for the professional breeder, awards gained at the big shows are a valuable recommendation, and could affect the price of subsequent pups.

Breed specifications can be quite strict, establishing the exact posture of the legs and head, colouring or shape of ears, tail and feet. Above all, the dog should be in peak condition, with a glossy, well-groomed coat, healthy teeth and gums, bright eyes and a lively but completely obedient nature. The dog will be examined thoroughly by the expert judges, both standing and walking, to ascertain that it moves correctly and will obey simple commands.

Many breeds must be clipped or trimmed in a certain way to be elegible in their class. Poodles, for example, once had to be 'Lion' or 'English Saddle' clipped for showing – the hindquarters being completely shaved

to show off the muscles, also the legs and tail, leaving a pom-pom effect. There are more modern clips producing topknots, bracelets and pom-poms. Specialist grooming, such as this, often has to be carried out by a professional.

At the small local shows, classes are more likely to be for 'dog most like its owner', 'prettiest bitch' or 'dog with most character', allowing scope for mongrels and cross-breeds to win prizes. This kind of show might be purely for fun, but your dog should still be entered in the best possible condition.

Left: The judges give the dog a thorough check all over. They will examine joints, muscles, hindquarters and teeth, as well as assessing its temperament. No aspect of the dog's physique or behaviour is missed and any flaws or faults are noted.

Left: It is always a proud moment when your dog wins its class: this 'Westie' has gone one better and come out top as Best in Show at Crufts.

Below: The dog's body shape and characteristics can be shown to best advantage by adjusting posture to balance head and tail.

Above: In the Dobermann, the judges will be looking for good straight legs, a well-set body, long lean head and dark eyes.

Below: Some owners specialize in keeping a certain breed and will raise their own litters to perfect the required characteristics.

Below: A 'lion clip' used to be compulsory for showing poodles. To conform, the hind legs had to be clipped, leaving bracelets that were in proportion to the size of the dog. The lower part of the tail was shaved, leaving a pom-pom at the top.

THE HEALTHY DOG

A healthy, happy dog is bright-eyed and energetic, with a good, glossy coat. But you cannot rely on regular grooming alone to keep your dog that way. Correct diet is essential for energy and general health. For this reason, feeding your dog table scraps alone is not a good idea. An adequate amount of fresh air and exercise is equally important to keep a dog fit and healthy, and this will naturally depend on its size and breed. A large or energetic type of dog, such as a Great Dane or Springer Spaniel, requires plenty of space for daily exercise. The tiny fluffy toy Papillon, by contrast, is a lively dog that can exercise quite happily within the confines of the average apartment, yet has the stamina to take longer walks outdoors.

Hygiene is a vital rule of good health: not just brushing and washing your dog, but also a regular check for disease and common problems so that they can be treated promptly. Teeth tend to be prone to tartar, causing bad breath and gum damage, and must be referred to a veterinarian. Ears should be checked weekly for ear mange, awkwardly growing tufts of hair and any foreign bodies, then cleaned with antiseptic. Dogs with long or folded ears need special checking. At the same time, check the eyes and remove any discharge that collects in the inner corner with cotton wool and sterilized water. Some breeds, such as toy dogs, are prone to redness and watery eyes; check

Above: Like any human patient, a dog will respond positively if you make a little fuss of it when it is feeling unwell or miserable.

with your veterinarian if this occurs. Examine the paws frequently to make sure nothing is lodged in the pad or between the toes. Nails may need clipping if your dog does not walk on hard surfaces very often. And don't forget to book an annual visit to the veterinarian for those routine inoculations – they could save your dog's life and prevent unnecessary suffering.

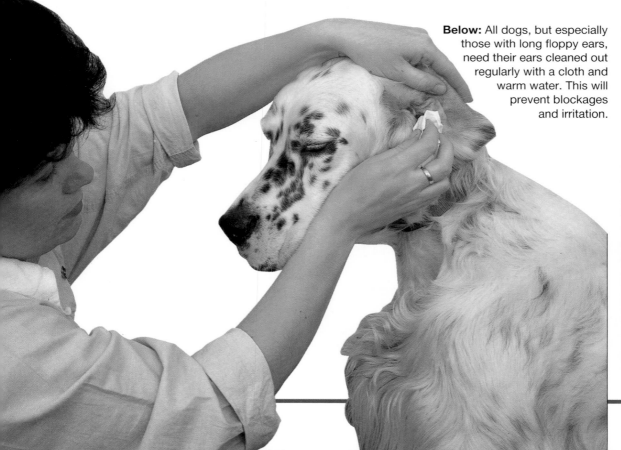

Below: All dogs, but especially those with long floppy ears, need their ears cleaned out regularly with a cloth and warm water. This will prevent blockages and irritation.

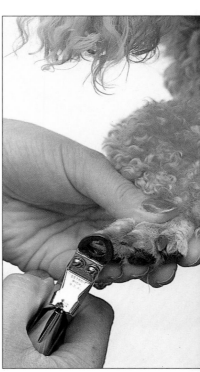

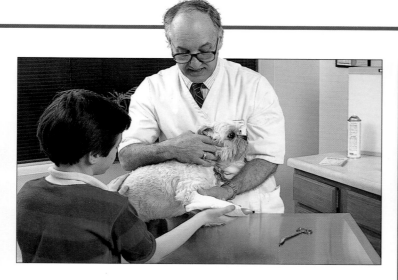

Above: If a dog has broken a bone, it needs to be expertly bandaged to ensure that the fracture heals correctly.

Below: The teeth play an important part in a dog's life and need to be checked regularly for signs of possible decay.

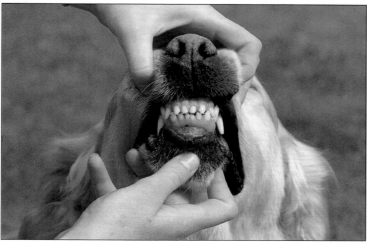

Above: Checking a dog's eyes is a difficult task to tackle single-handed, so it is a good idea to have an assistant standing by to hold the animal steady while carrying out the examination.

Below: Sometimes the eyes become clogged and begin to close up. Remedy this as promptly as possible, using a lint-free swab of clean warm water.

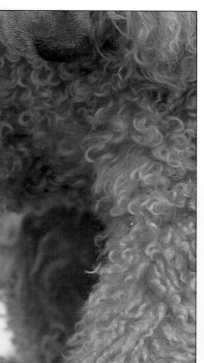

Left: Clipping the nails regularly will help the dog to walk without any undue pain or discomfort. Remember that dew-claws do not wear down; left unclipped, they curve and dig into the flesh.

A GENTLE COMPANION

Hopefully, any dog chosen as a pet will be good fun and friendly, as happy as its owner to romp, play or simply be companionable. If they are well cared for and contented, most dogs are enthusiastic, loyal and affectionate friends. Common sense should prevent you from choosing a breed specifically trained as a ferocious guard dog to be a family pet.

Some dogs are specially bred for their supreme good nature and friendliness. They are expensive, but their character can be virtually guaranteed from puppyhood. Certain breeds are renowned for their gentleness and tolerance, making them an excellent choice for households with young children or for older people who want a quiet, easily managed companion. Many of the dogs that come into this category are among the larger dogs, which seem to have that strong, silent attitude, whereas smaller breeds are often excitable, and sometimes snappy. The Komondor looks like a huge friendly hearth rug and, although a good and powerful watchdog, is very gentle with children. The big, curly Leonberger is another gentle giant – a fine watchdog, but devoted to the younger members of the household. The great, shaggy Newfoundland is equally famous for these traits.

Sometimes, a quiet peaceable nature is useful in other environments, outside the family home. The Hanoverian Schweisshund is popular as a hunting dog, having an excellent sense of smell, and a patient tranquil nature for stalking and sitting out game. The Flat-coated and Golden Retriever and the Clumber Spaniel are other sporting dogs renowned for their good nature, which has also made them popular family pets. There is also at least one small dog that is always gentle, intelligent and charming: the Japanese Chin, a dainty dog with a pretty plumed tail.

Below: Underneath its rather fierce shaggy appearance, the Bouvier de Flandres is a quiet, good-tempered and gentle dog.

Below: The Brittany Spaniel is not only a fine sporting dog, but also a particularly good-natured and enjoyable companion. In return for its loyalty, it looks for kindness.

Left: The Golden Retriever is an affectionate gundog or pet and very good with children. Give it regular daily exercise.

Above: The Newfoundland is famous the world over for its massive size, gentle nature, reliability and unfailing devotion.

Below: Obedient and extremely patient, Golden Retrievers are much sought-after, both as hunting dogs and family pets.

Above: Another big shaggy dog with a heart of gold – the Leonberger from Germany – becomes devoted to its owner.

Below: A faithful, well-behaved dog is a source of pride and a pleasure to be with at all times.

FAMILIAR FRIENDS

Some breeds of dog go in and out of fashion, challenging the breeders to keep up with changing demand. Others seem to be perennial favourites. It is difficult to identify just what it is that makes a dog consistently popular and well loved. It is obviously not simply a good appearance – look at the Basset Hound's sad wrinkles – but it could be a friendly temperament or simply a traditional love of a particular breed. The Jack Russell Terrier, not even recognized as an official breed, is a lively and clever companion. This useful small dog is a keen hunter of large vermin, and intelligent enough to be taught a wide range of tricks.

Other small dogs that have become all-time favourites must include the Corgi. It was once a cattle dog, but its popularity as a pet and show dog has refined its rough, aggressive nature – although it may still be quick with a sharp nip. Curious in appearance, but still loved, is the Dachshund, with its long, sausagelike body and short legs. Despite its small size and its popularity as a town and city pet, the Dachshund is a brave hunter, prized for its digging ability. There are about six recognized breeds, including smooth-haired and long-haired types. The hairy Scottish Terrier, or 'Scottie', is another small muscular hunting dog that has become a favourite pet, full of character. The bigger breeds are equally popular: from the shaggy Old English Sheepdog, with its amazing long coat and affectionate nature, to the long-nosed, intelligent Collie (Rough or Smooth) and similar, but smaller, Sheltie, or Shetland Sheepdog, with its lovely mixture of coat colours.

Right: The much-loved Basset Hound, with its low-slung body and drooping features, proves that you do not have to be handsome to be popular.

Below: The Long-haired Dachshund is particularly attractive, with its long silky coat and feathered tail and legs. The Miniature Dachshund has long been a particular favourite.

Left: Originally a working dog, the Old English Sheepdog now makes a good guard dog, as well as an affectionate and easily trained family pet.

Below: The spotted Dalmatian is often the choice of someone looking for a stylish pet. Despite its short coat, it requires daily grooming, as the fur does shed.

Above: Bulldogs are funny-looking but lovable – their courage and loyalty, combined with a compact size and strong constitution make them a good pet. Bear in mind that they do tend to dribble rather a lot.

Below: The Jack Russell Terrier has endeared itself to thousands of dog owners for many years. They appreciate its small size, lively mischievous nature and the quick intelligence that enables it to learn tricks.

Left: The intelligent and faithful Rough Collie must have plenty of exercise and enjoys being busy. However, it is happy enough indoors, so it does make a good house dog. It is a fine guard dog and was originally bred as a sheepdog in Scotland.

LOVABLE SPANIELS

From obedient and efficient gundog to faithful and affectionate pet, it is hard not to love spaniels, with their liquid eyes, soft ears and fine silky coat. They are generally excellent sporting dogs, willing to retrieve from rough ground or water, and equally good at tracking and holding game. The mouth is strong and muscular, and the coat silky but slightly oily, to repel water, burrs and tangles.

The English Springer Spaniel is said to be the oldest of the sporting spaniels. It was once used to spring, or flush, birds into the open or into waiting nets, and used to be divided into two types: land and water spaniels. Today's breed probably evolved from the original land spaniel. The Welsh Springer Spaniel is very close to pictures of such dogs in eighteenth century prints. An excellent working dog, it is smaller than the English Springer and larger than the Cocker, an equally good dog for a country home or city apartment, providing it has plenty of exercise. Cocker Spaniels are now used less frequently as sporting dogs, but their compactness, feathery coat and lovely variety of colours make them a charming pet. The American Cocker Spaniel has particularly fine markings and a long silky coat that needs a lot of grooming, making it a popular show dog. Smallest of the spaniels is the King Charles Spaniel, compact and well proportioned, with long feathery ears, large dark eyes and an attractive choice of coat colours, from the Black and Tan to the rich Ruby.

Right: Somewhat smaller than the English Cocker Spaniel from which it was originally bred last century, the American breed retains the same attractive silky coat and lively alert expression.

Above: American Cocker Spaniels have been recognized as a separate breed since the 1930s and are hugely popular as a pet dog in North America.

Above: Clean and compact, the English Cocker Spaniel makes an excellent house pet. Bear in mind that it will soon get fat if overfed and under exercised.

Above: The Irish Water Spaniel is primarily a hunting dog, ideally suited to tracking wild duck on marshes and lakes. Its short oily coat and webbed toes are valuable assets in the water.

Left: The English Cocker Spaniel is both an energetic sporting dog and a lively small companion. It has long soft ears and a thick silky coat that is seen in a wide variety of colours.

Right: Although smaller than the more familiar English breed, Welsh Springer Spaniels are equally friendly pets and an excellent sporting dog. They are hard working and tolerant.

Right: The Clumber Spaniel takes its name from Clumber Park in England, where this compact, friendly and reliable breed was originally developed.

ELEGANT AND EXOTIC

Certain dogs are guaranteed to turn heads: walking haughtily on the end of a leash, leaping gracefully across the grass or through the trees, they have an exaggerated sleekness of body shape, from the end of their long pointed snout to the limits of a whiplike or plumelike tail. They move seemingly effortlessly on the longest of legs. Their head is held proudly at all times and their eye has a distinctly arrogant air. Many are related to the old greyhound-type of dog worshipped by the Ancient Egyptians, and depicted in wall paintings and sculptures dated 4,000 B.C. The Pharaoh Hound is certainly one such descendant. This small, speedy hound is almost identical to pictures of the dog-god Anubis, as is the Ibizan Hound, a Spanish hunting greyhound with attractive white, red and fawn colouring.

If the elegant body shape is further refined, you will have a Whippet, a dog that looks as fragile as a leaf, but which is, in reality, a strong muscular animal that makes a fine sporting and racing dog, as well as a good pet. Equally noble in appearance – and an excellent hunting dog – is the sand-coloured Sloughi. It is not surprising that this particular dog is so beautiful and noble in appearance, for it is the result of a strict breeding plan that deliberately eliminated any weak or imperfect puppies. More exotic still is the related Saluki, a graceful hunter, with long silky ears and a feathery tail; or the slender Borzoi, which has beautiful wavy, silky hair and the slightly arched back that gives these dogs such an air of disdain.

Above: Arabian nomads once used the sleek Sloughi to hunt gazelle and hare, and it still retains a lean body and exceptional speed, both resulting from strict breeding.

Right: The Ibizan Hound is a form of Spanish Greyhound, with a long narrow head and lean level body. Males have a tendency to fight and their natural aggressiveness may make them difficult to train.

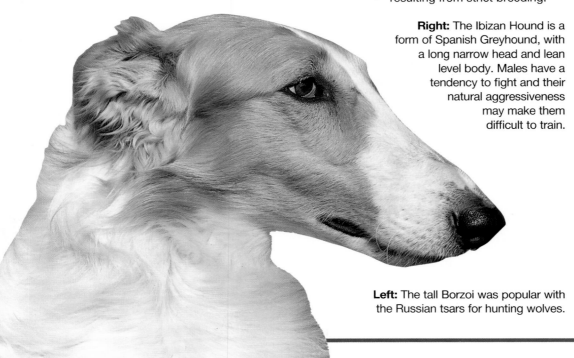

Left: The tall Borzoi was popular with the Russian tsars for hunting wolves.

Above: Extremely slender and streamlined, the lightweight Whippet is designed to move with great grace and speed.

Right: The beautiful and elegant Afghan Hound has a wonderfully long silky coat and exuberant affectionate nature.

Below right: These cuddly Saluki pups will grow into large graceful dogs, with liquid almond-shaped eyes, long silky ears and a feathered tail.

ARISTOCRATS AMONG DOGS

As soon as a member of a royal family takes a fancy to a particular breed, it gives the dog a special status and popularity. Kings of most centuries have kept packs of their preferred hunting dogs, while their queens and the grand ladies of the court liked pet lap dogs and toy breeds, such as Maltese and Bolognese Bichons. Sometimes, the court would be so keen on a particular breed or a royal personage became so fond of a dog that they would give their name to the breed. During the reigns of King Charles I and King Charles II in the UK, one particular dog was so popular that it became known as the King Charles Spaniel. This appealing dog probably originated in China and was very popular in France and the rest of Europe, before being adopted by the English around about the sixteenth century. But it was in the seventeenth century, under the reign of King Charles II, that these stocky black-and-tan dogs, with their large melting eyes and long feathery ears, became so loved by the king that they were known as 'Charlies'. Later, three other varieties were developed: the black-tan-and-white Prince Charles, an all-chestnut called a Ruby, and the chestnut-and-white Blenheim.

Other breeds of dog might be recognized as aristocrats because of their noble and striking appearance, as well as on account of some past royal approval. The haughty Borzoi was a favourite with the crowned heads of Russia, as well as with Queen Victoria. Another well-known breed, the Italian Greyhound, has also been kept among the aristocracy for many years, either for hunting purposes, or simply for the elegance of its lithe body. You will often see them depicted in paintings, at the feet of their owner or lying down gracefully by the fireplace.

Below: The King Charles Spaniel got its name from its popularity as a pet during the reign of King Charles II, but it was once a sporting dog that hunted in packs. Cross-breeding has now bred out its hunting inclinations.

Right: The Borzoi has an aristocratic look – tall and haughty, with a long tapering muzzle. Originally used for hunting wolves, it later became a popular royal pet.

Above: The Shih Tzu was once considered a sacred animal in China and exporting them to other countries was forbidden.

Above: At one time, the tiny Papillon, less than 28cm(11in) tall, was a fashion accessory in the royal courts of Europe.

Above: The Afghan's height, flat back, long ears and muzzle give it a suitably aristocratic air. However, this ancient breed was primarily a desert hunting dog and needs plenty of exercise.

GOOD GUARD DOGS

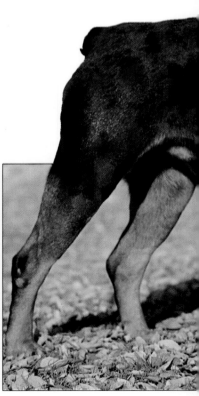

The best guard dogs are strong and obedient. They tend to belong to the bigger, more intelligent breeds that can be rigorously trained and controlled. To anyone other than their handler, they can be frightening and formidable opponents, trained to bring a person down as speedily and fiercely as possible. Training should start when the animal is young.

Some dogs are naturally aggressive, and these are the ones chosen for training as guards. Rottweilers are solid and muscular, yet surprisingly nimble. They were originally used to protect the money purses of travelling German butchers as they drove their cattle to market, and were subsequently known as 'The Butcher's Dog of Rottweil'. The German Shepherd Dog, popular since the 1920s, is an attractive faithful breed, with a wide range of talents, making it a good guide dog and pet, as well as an efficient guard dog. In Turkey, the white-coated Kuvasz is an excellent guard and hunting dog, tireless and easily trained. Its name comes from the Turkish word 'to guard' and these dogs are popular both with the military and the police.

Once a fierce fighting dog, the talents of the Neapolitan Mastiff have more recently been turned towards guard duties, particularly by the Italian police, but these dogs can be dangerous if not properly

Right: The bright and obedient Keeshond was a popular guard dog aboard the Dutch barges on the canals.

controlled. Another fighter turned guard dog is the Dogue de Bordeaux, but years of breeding have encouraged a gentler nature without any loss of its excellent guard dog abilities. The Boxer and Bull Mastiff are two other ferocious-looking breeds popular as watchdogs, yet have a gentler side to their nature.

Below: Naturally playful and strong, the Boxer must be trained with a firm hand to control its rather boisterous tendencies. However, once trained, its loyal and affectionate nature makes this athletic, intelligent breed an excellent family watchdog. Give it plenty of regular outdoor exercise.

Below: Alert and obedient, the strong Rottweiler makes a fierce guard dog that needs firm training and expert handling.

Above: The Dobermann Pinscher is naturally aggressive from an early age, and can be a daunting sight with teeth bared. This tendency, combined with a loyal and obedient nature, can result in a top-class guard dog when trained.

Right: The German Shepherd Dog is one of the most popular guard dog breeds in the world, with its strong muscular body, excellent intelligence and natural agility.

Below: The solidly built Mastiff is another aggressive breed that needs firm handling. It has been a popular and well respected guard dog since at least Roman times, and has proved both brave and loyal.

WORKING DOGS

Wherever you may go, you will always find dogs of one sort or another, some highly bred for a particular purpose, others, perhaps, still half-crossed with the local wolf or wild dog population. Most often you will find working dogs; long ago, man adapted the dog to suit his needs and then found it indispensable.

Dogs have the strength and intelligence to carry out so many different tasks that we would find it difficult to manage without them. Imagine a hill shepherd trying to control the sheep or return an escaped ewe to the rest of the flock without the help of a dog, or dogs. Farm dogs can be trained to various standards, using either hand and spoken commands or a whistle. The dogs used for this sort of job vary according to country or terrain. The Border Collie is ideally bred for the rough borderlands between England and Scotland, but is equally popular in Australia.

Dogs also play an important role as man's companion in hunting, helping to track injured game or steering the prey into the sights of a waiting huntsman. Where foxes pose a threat, dogs may play an important role in stock management, too. Gamekeepers, security guards and policemen all rely on dogs to guard and protect both themselves and valuable goods or even other animals in their care.

Below: The rough, hairy Briard is an excellent French sheepdog, with a lovable nature and boundless energy.

It is quite amazing that a dog can be trained for so many different tasks, depending on a breed's particular skill. It may be pulling heavy sleds across the Arctic, hunting for truffles or helping the blind. It could be sniffing out and tracking, locating people buried underground, detecting drugs or explosives, or controlling crowds. Dogs are surely the most versatile of all creatures and will always be looked upon as man's best workmate.

Right: Originally trained to hunt large game, the Boxer is an excellent and obedient watch dog. It needs plenty of exercise.

Below: The German Giant Schnauzer, with its distinctive bushy moustache, is an easy-to-train, sturdy cattle dog breed.

Above: The truffle-hunting dogs of France's Perigord region are essential for retrieving these delicacies. The fungal growths develop underground and the dogs locate them by smell.

Left: The Bloodhound has the reputation of being the best breed of dog for tracking, due to its keen sense of smell. It is still valued by police forces to assist them in their investigative work.

Below: A good sheepdog will learn to pen sheep simply in response to messages from its master by mouth or whistle. These dogs often achieve considerable success in obedience tests.

Below: Until the last century, Collies were an ancient Scottish sheep-guarding breed. Today, they are popular watchdogs.

BUILT FOR SPEED

Some dogs have the ability to surprise, moving with unexpected quickness and agility, despite a slow solid-looking build. This can be particularly true of many guard breeds. However, a dog specially refined for speed – it may have been bred for hunting or racing – is immediately recognizable by its lithe greyhound-type body, delicately arched back, and a build so lean that almost every rib and sinew is visible. The Greyhound is one of the oldest and purest breeds, prized for thousands of years as a fleet and sure-footed hunter, and later as a first-class racing dog. The Whippet looks like a miniature Greyhound, but is, in fact, quite different, having a shorter body and longer, wider head. It remains lean as a bone, and is extremely fast, both on the track and in the field. The Pharaoh Hound is related to the ancient Greyhound; its lithe body and strong muscular legs give it great speed and agility. There are also some large dogs renowned for their tremendous speed and surprising agility that have been bred mainly for hunting. These include the large but powerful Deerhound, its sleek greyhound roots clearly visible beneath a rough grey-blue or brindled coat, and the beautiful Saluki, which looks far

too gentle and elegant to have the kind of speed and endurance necessary to hunt gazelle, fox and hare across the inhospitable desert. Even the beautiful Afghan, with its long silky hair and cultured style, was once a keen hunter of wolves and leopards.

Above: These lively Whippet pups will reach maturity at about two years old, but their lean shape is already evident here.

Left: Wild game has gradually disappeared from the desert and thus the Saluki's traditional role has changed. Once a fast and efficient hunter, today it has become a show winner.

Above: Seen in action, the Afghan becomes a sleek and powerful speed machine. Its agility and long flowing coat were originally well suited to mountain weather and terrain.

Left: Fastest of all the dogs for its size, the Whippet can easily attain speeds of 55kph(35mph). Yet this is a breed with a quiet and affectionate nature that makes it an excellent house pet, providing you can give it plenty of daily exercise.

Above: In the UK, the muscular Greyhound is still regarded primarily as a racing dog. It is capable of attaining speeds of 70kph(43.5mph) on the track.

Below: Although still used by the Afghani nomads as a hunting and shepherd dog, the Afghan Hound makes a fine, if spirited, friend and show dog.

TENACIOUS TERRIERS

Terriers have a long history of hunting and fighting, and are renowned as tough tireless dogs with an irresistible sense of fun. From the Airedale – a big, powerful dog – to the delicate smooth-coated Manchester Terrier, these are dogs with a huge amount of character. Most are distinguished by a rough or curly coat that requires clipping at least once a year to keep it looking trim, otherwise the wiry hair can become ragged.

The Airedale is large enough to be an excellent dog for police and guard work, but generally, terriers are small plucky dogs that enjoy hunting vermin and small mammals far larger than themselves. Most were bred as working or hunting dogs, such as the rough Border Terrier, an efficient foxhunter from the borders between England and Scotland. Another well-valued, working terrier is the Lakeland Terrier, often employed to keep down the fox population in northern, sheep-farming country. The Fox Terrier earned its name from its speed and endurance in keeping up with the foxhound pack, and was once a popular hunting dog. Ironically, it is now purely a valued pet and companion that has adapted to the city as well as to the country.

Some terriers have been specially bred for city life, their small size and appealing character making them attractive and popular pets. The Scottish Terrier, or 'Scottie', tends to be rather grumpy, but with its familiar stocky body, big moustache and black coat, remains a favourite. Its counterpart is the West Highland White – a far more cheerful dog. Its rough white coat repels dirt and dust, so that it always looks clean.

Right: Capable of tracking game as large as a bear or deer, the Airedale is the largest of the terrier breed, and a popular, faithful guard dog.

Below: Peering out from its long wiry coat, the small Skye Terrier makes a good pet for city apartments, as it requires little exercise. It was once a Highland working dog.

Below: The Wire-haired Fox Terrier has an alert intelligent expression, even as a pup. However, it can become over-excited and aggressive if not handled firmly. Although once a popular hunting dog, it is now kept as a house pet.

Above: It is believed that the Tibetan Terrier was once bred by Tibetan monks as a symbol of good luck. It is an affectionate and easily trained small pet, but requires a good brushing daily.

Right: The Silky Terrier is a small Australian dog, compact enough to suit flat or apartment owners, but with a noisy and aggressive bark, which makes it an effective guard dog.

Below: Bull Terriers were once bred as fierce fighting dogs and although they now have a much sweeter nature, they require a strong hand to keep them out of mischief.

Above: Strong and spirited for its size, the little West Highland White Terrier makes a lively and entertaining companion, but it tends to shed its hair a lot and requires regular grooming.

DOGS FOR SNOW

We know the spitz type of dog as the 'Husky'. Its thick double coat, strong muscular body, and tightly curled tail (to protect paws and nose when resting), enable it to withstand the worst Arctic weather. In fact, this is one of the earliest domesticated dogs, and is one of a wide range of breeds that are still specially adapted to the cold and snow. The Elkhound is equally typical, its dense coat making it perfectly suited to working in a cold climate; once used to hunt bear and reindeer, it is still used to track and restrain elk (moose) in Norway. Another hardworking snow dog of the spitz type is the lovely Samoyed – again usually all-white – and with a most attractive, smiling expression. The Samoyed is a good all-round snow dog, capable of pulling a sledge, hunting small animals or guarding an encampment. Even their thick, dense coat may be spun and woven into warm clothes.

Other breeds are specially suited to sled-pulling and have a highly developed pack instinct, as well as a better coverage of fur – even on the underbelly – to avoid frostbite. The Siberian Husky, for example, still has a lot of wolf in its temperament and is an excellent pack dog, pulling with speed and stamina. It is widely used for sled racing. There is another type of dog specially adapted to cold, snowy conditions – the mountain dog. These include the surprisingly sure-footed Saint Bernard, the powerful all-white Pyrenean Mountain Dog and the golden Leonberger. These friendly, obedient, big dogs are excellent protection for mountain-grazed animals and famous for their ability to rescue lost climbers and walkers.

Left: The Siberian Husky is probably the best-known Arctic sled dog, although the term 'husky' may be applied to any sled-pulling breed. It is an attractive dog, with a powerful head, striking markings and excellent pack instincts.

Right: The Pyrenean Mountain Dog is a large and handsome breed, with a thick white coat and friendly face. Although gentle and obedient, its intelligence and stamina make it a valuable mountain sheepdog in the Pyrenees.

Above: A thick coat and tough constitution enable the Eskimo Dog to survive with little food in the bitterest weather. In the Canadian Arctic it is used for hunting and sled pulling.

Above: One of the very best pack breeds, Siberian Husky dogs are friendly and affectionate and do not tend to fight when pulling sleds as a team. Isolation has kept the breed naturally pure.

Right: The large friendly Saint Bernard, with its flask of reviving brandy around the neck, is traditionally associated with the Swiss Alps. It is an essential member of mountain rescue teams.

Above: The Samoyed is a thick-coated spitz breed, native to Siberia, where it was originally bred for sled-pulling, hunting game and herding reindeer. Its ability to survive the harshest climate, a keen sense of smell and its great strength and endurance have made it a useful snow rescue dog. Samoyeds accompanied Nansen, the explorer, to the North Pole.

SPORTING DOGS

Dogs may be known as man's best friend, but for the huntsman and sportsman they can be his perfect teammates too. Quick, tireless legs and a keen sense of smell mean game can be easily located and retrieved. Some specially developed breeds of gundog, such as spaniels and pointers, are good dual-purpose dogs: they will both retrieve and 'point' – that is, locate sitting birds and indicate their position by freezing and looking intently at the appropriate spot. Others are noted for their particular aptitude to one of these tasks. As their name suggests, retrievers are excellent at tracking and collecting wounded game. They need a powerful muzzle to bring back large waterfowl and hares, but a soft mouth so that the skin of the quarry is never pierced.

Certain breeds are valued for their willingness to retrieve from water as well as land. The tough Chesapeake Bay Retriever is expert at fetching duck from the icy waters of Chesapeake Bay, USA. The worldwide Labrador Retriever is also bred to work in water and was originally used by fishermen to take fish-laden nets ashore. Other dogs excel at pointing and 'setting': crouching or sitting motionless when they scent a bird. The strong Italian Spinone, with its rough, patchy coat, is renowned for its hypnotic stare, while the Gordon Setter, a Scottish gundog, is probably best at its job of all the setter breeds.

Right: Powerful and sleek, the Labrador is an excellent water dog, capable of retrieving waterfowl from a river or lake, even in icy conditions. It is equally efficient on dry land and in woodland.

There are several breeds of dog that prefer to hunt in packs and their popularity for foot- or horse-hunted sport such as fox, hare and stag, has remained undiminished for centuries. Sturdy Foxhounds, Beagles and Harriers are enthusiastic and obedient dogs, able to keep up with the chase all day. Do bear in mind that gundogs tend to be happiest with an active outdoor life and do not make good town dogs.

Left: The Chesapeake Bay Retriever is a superb water dog, specially bred for its coarse, oily coat that will endure the worst conditions. Popular in the USA.

Above: Taking its name from the Celtic word 'beag' meaning small, the Beagle is the smallest of the English pack hounds. It is a robust and healthy animal.

Above left: A well-trained sporting dog is totally obedient and will sit patiently or come to heel promptly on command. You must begin its training early on.

Above: The German Short-haired Pointer is a good all-round gundog, tracking game and marking out quarry on any kind of terrain. An obedient dog.

Left: Foxhounds have excellent stamina and will keep up with the hunt all day whatever the weather and the terrain covered.

Above: Largest of the setters, the Gordon Setter is a good-natured hunting dog.

Right: If well trained from an early age, this young Weimaraner will grow up to be an efficient, well-behaved all-purpose sporting dog, good for big game hunting.

Left: Once the dog has retrieved the game, it should not drop it until told to do so. Normally, it will patiently await further instructions.

BIG GAME DOGS

Certain dogs are skilled and well equipped to hunt and catch much bigger game. The Irish Wolfhound is no longer required to track and hunt wolves, and few dogs are still required to kill bears, but there are still large breeds that are a valuable, and sometimes necessary, companion to those keen on hunting big game. Many have their specialist areas. The Elkhound's name is self explanatory, this spitz-type dog also tracks badger, bear, deer and lynx in its native Norway. The Akita is an attractive Japanese dog, used most successfully to hunt deer and wild boar. The African Basenji will point, retrieve and drive game, and is unusual in that it does not bark, but produces instead a curious, yodelling sound.

Some breeds are in danger of disappearing now that their particular skills are no longer in demand. The aristocratic-looking Bleu de Gascogne was once prized for its ability to hunt wolves, although it is equally skilled at coursing hare and deer. It looks very like the American Bluetick Coonhound, and remains a dependable and fast hunter, despite a recent drop in popularity. The Griffon Nivernais is still valued for the strength and endurance that made it such an excellent wild boar hunter. Some dogs will even face the most ferocious of quarries: the Rhodesian Ridgeback fearlessly hunts lions and other big game, tracking them down in packs before driving them towards the guns. Their nickname is 'lionhound' from their fearless habit of holding a lion at bay by growling and snarling until the owner can reach the scene.

Right: Descended from a South African hunting dog, the Rhodesian Ridgeback takes its name from a curious crest of hair that grows along the centre of the back in an opposite direction to the rest of its coat. It was established in Rhodesia by early pioneers who crossed the breed with Great Danes and other large breeds to increase its size and strength. It is fierce and fearless, and used for hunting big game, such as lions.

Above: The enormously tall, yet surprisingly docile, Irish Wolfhound was indeed once used to hunt wolves. When wolves became largely extinct in the eighteenth century, the number of wolfhounds naturally declined as well, but this strong rough-haired dog is now popular as an oversized pet.

Right: The intelligent and alert Basenji is distinguished by the fact that it does not bark, although it does emit a kind of chuckling yodel noise. The high-set tail curls over to one side of the back. It is also noted as a curiosity by its trotting gait; however, this does not affect its excellent qualities as a fine hunting dog in its native Africa.

Left: Unmistakably one of the spitz type of dogs, and thus ideally suited to snowy conditions, the Elkhound's superb sense of smell and stamina make it a valuable ally in Norway for hunting elk, reindeer and other large game. Its appearance remains little changed since the Stone Age.

Below: The Japanese Akita is a quiet obedient dog, with a strong compact body and attractive thick coat. Its fine appearance belies a brave and eager nature. It is not difficult to train and, although capable of hunting even black bears, these days it is more likely to be used for hunting deer and wild boar.

GIANTS OF THE DOG WORLD

Below: Large but gentle, the tawny Leonberger may be a cross between Newfoundlands and Saint Bernards.

The Irish Wolfhound is one of the biggest dogs in the world. Measuring up to 98cm(38in) tall and covered in thick, rather rough-looking hair, it is an impressive sight, guaranteed to startle everyone – even those who are familiar with the breed. Like most big dogs, the Irish Wolfhound can be remarkably docile and, like many other large breeds, is loved for its character, as well as for its dramatic good looks.

Several giant breeds make wonderful pets and delightful companions, if you have the space to keep them and the time to exercise them. The huge hairy Newfoundland is a favourite with children, as well as an excellent rescue dog. Equally reliable and attractive, in a large solid way, is the white-coated Kuvasz. Designed to survive in cold, bleak climates, the Pyrenean Mountain Dog is easily identified by its long, thick, coarse white coat and gentle, obedient nature.

Over-sized but cuddly, some dogs seem instantly appealing and are long-standing favourites. The Old English Sheepdog peers out from a thick shaggy coat of grey-blue or white and black hair. Equally bearlike, but with a rough bushy white coat to the ground is the Komondor from Hungary, another breed originally trained to protect the flocks from harm. Less cosy, perhaps, but just as stunning in size is the solidly built Mastiff. It remains popular, largely as a guard dog. The German Mastiff, or Great Dane, has a more elegant but equally muscular body, and is a giant, standing at 76cm(30in). Another distinguished, straight-standing giant is the Francais Blanc et Noir – a handsome black-and-white hunting dog from France.

Below: Great Danes are large and muscular, with erect ears and drooping jowls. They require plenty of food and outdoor exercise.

Above: Although famous as a mountain rescue dog, the shaggy Saint Bernard, with its loyal and patient nature, also makes a good family pet.

Right: Big dogs often combine great strength and size with a protective, docile nature. These qualities make them ideal companions for young children.

Above: The huge and powerful Irish Wolfhound has rough wiry hair in a choice of colours from grey and white to fawn, rust and even black. Despite its size and vigour, the pups can be difficult to rear and need special care.

Below: The Kuvasz is a large Turkish guard dog, widely used by both shepherds and the military. In fact, its name means 'guard' in Turkish. Easily trained and good natured, the Kuvasz also makes a fine and reliable, if sizeable, family pet.

Right: The Briard, or Berger de Brie, is a large shaggy Belgian working dog, now used mainly as a guard dog and guide dog, as well as being a popular pet.

SMALL DOGS FOR SMALL HOMES

Big dogs are for people with big homes, who like the outdoors and who enjoy plenty of exercise in all weathers. These dogs are boisterous, great fun, but exhausting. One of the smaller breeds is a far more practical proposition if you have a minimum of time or energy to spare, live in an apartment or simply prefer an animal that you can hold on your lap and stroke. For this reason, some of the classic small breeds remain immensely popular and are automatically some people's first choice – if the dog dies, they usually replace it with one from the same breed.

Poodles are especially intelligent and good fun, (although there is a much larger, hunting poodle) and are perennial favourites, with their tightly curled coats and entertaining nature. Equally popular is the Dachshund, with its funny long, low body and little legs, or the stockier Corgi. The dog need not be beautiful to be much in demand, and many of the smaller breeds are far from elegant. Consider the English Bulldog that looks like a little barrel on square set legs and has the ugliest, squashed face imaginable. The Pug is not much more handsome, small and squat with a face like a piece of sooty choux pastry, and a tightly curled tail. Even the West Highland White or Cairn Terriers are a bit too rough and bewhiskered to be considered truly handsome. However, some breeds are very attractive and greatly appealing: the

Cocker Spaniel with its great liquid eyes; or the glossy Miniature Pinscher, dainty as a small deer. Other dogs are clipped, trimmed or even dyed to suit their owner's desire, especially the long-suffering Poodle.

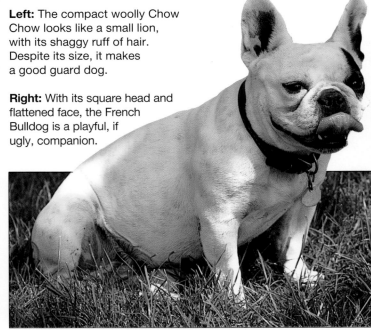

Left: The compact woolly Chow Chow looks like a small lion, with its shaggy ruff of hair. Despite its size, it makes a good guard dog.

Right: With its square head and flattened face, the French Bulldog is a playful, if ugly, companion.

Above: There are six different breeds of Dachshund, including this rougher looking wire-hair. Its coat keeps out cold and rain.

Above: Once a fierce bull baiter, today's stocky English Bulldog is a good-tempered and popular dog. It is quick to learn and fond of children.

Above: The Jack Russell Terrier is a lively and highly intelligent dog that has enjoyed immense popularity for many years, but it is not officially recognized by the Kennel Club as a pedigree.

Left: Although small, the Welsh Corgi requires plenty of exercise. It makes a lively and affectionate pet.

Below: Highly fashionable in the eighteenth and nineteenth centuries, the squat Pug can be clever and amusing, but is not always good tempered.

Below: Originally an excellent gundog, the Poodle's partially clipped coat was once a practical measure for swimming. It is a good retriever and fond of water, if allowed a dip.

MINIATURE LAP DOGS

The smallest ornamental dogs were regarded almost as ornaments and bred as such. The fine ladies of the court would enjoy slipping them into their sleeves or handbags, petting them on their laps or taking them for walks on tiny golden chains. This was a popular practice in Europe from as early as the fifteenth century – in Ancient China and Japan, the practice goes back centuries earlier.

Some lap dogs are miniature versions of larger breeds. There are miniature and toy Poodles, for example, a miniature long-haired Dachshund and even a miniature form of the Pinscher - little bigger than a Chihuahua at only 30cm(12in) in height. The smallest breed of dog in the world, the Chihuahua, is hardly bigger than a large rodent, measuring only 16-20cm(6-8in) high, and can have either a smooth, shiny coat or a long silky one. Equally popular as a toy breed is the Yorkshire Terrier, whose tiny body is invisible beneath a long, flowing coat of silky hair, usually tied on the head in a ribboned topknot. If kept for showing, this dog requires a great deal of special grooming. Very similar in looks is the much-loved Shih Tzu, with its mass of dense hair that prompted the Chinese to call it 'Lion-dog'; or the Lhasa Apso, whose thicker coat may be any one of a range of colours.

Another popular lap dog owes its origins to the remotest country in the world; the pretty and unusual-looking Tibetan Spaniel has a delicate appearance, with feathery ears and tail. The Papillon – a dog tiny and delicate enough for ladies in bygone days to carry in their muffs – also has big fringed ears like a butterfly ('papillon' means butterfly), and a feathery tail.

Below: The affectionate Pomeranian is the tiniest of the spitz breeds, but displays the classic plumed tail and long thick coat typical of its family.

Right: A small dog, such as this lovable Yorkshire Terrier, makes a fine companion for those who live in town and city apartments, but it also enjoys a country walk.

Left: Although it is a small and ornamental dog, with a lovely long coat, the ancient Lhasa Apso is capable of surviving the severe climate of its native Tibet. The coat needs daily grooming.

Above: The Tibetan Spaniel was not known in the West until earlier this century, but it has quickly become a much-loved lap dog, with its bright delicate features and adaptable nature.

Below: The long-coated Chihuahua was developed by crossing the smooth-coated animal with other small breeds, such as the Pomeranian.

Above: Looking little more than a ball of white fluff, the Bichon Frise is as popular now in Europe and North America as it was in sixteenth-century France. The silky coat needs to be kept expertly trimmed to maintain its soft curly appearance, and the dog bathed about once a month. A dog for an owner with plenty of time to spare.

Above: The Shih Tzu is another whiskery lap dog that looks more like a fluffy toy. It originated in China, where it is considered sacred – the name means lion dog. This is a dog that enjoys being spoiled, and it is well suited to life in a small apartment, but it also needs regular walks to stay fit.

Right: The smallest dog in the world, the Chihuahua, may weigh little more than 1kg(2.2lb) when fully grown, and can be long- or smooth-coated. Loving and loyal, it likes company and needs plenty of exercise.

CURIOSITIES OF THE DOG WORLD

Some dogs are big and woolly as bears – the Newfoundland, for example, with its massive head and dense flat hair. The Chow Chow looks more like a cuddly teddy bear or small lion, with its thick tawny mane and tiny catlike paws. The Mexican Hairless is unusual in a different way; it is more like a small rodent, and completely bald, with a slender graceful body, soft skin and pricked-up ears. These oddities among the dog world are prized, both as unusual pets and for showing, where every effort is made to refine their quirky appearance to perfection. The Bedlington Terrier looks like a young lamb, and its coat should be carefully clipped to emphasize the similarity. With its funny oval head and droopy ears, each ending in a tassel, the Bedlington is not as soft and defenceless as it looks – in fact, it is a good fighter and rabbit hunter. The Dandie Dinmont is another distinctive terrier. It has a long hairy body on little, short legs, and a bushy topknot of hair on its head. Its bark is surprisingly loud for so small a dog and it makes a good guard dog.

Some breeds are distinguished by their curious coats: the Komondor and Puli, for example, have a shaggy sheeplike fleece that disguises all their features. Other breeds have such comical squashed faces that it is impossible to resist a smile on seeing them – the Pug is a perennial favourite among these dogs. Less common is the Chinese Shar-Pei; its face and body are completely soft and crumpled, as if its skin is too large.

Above: The San Juan Teotihuacan is an extremely rare dog. It is believed that this ancient breed was once kept as a pet by the Aztecs. Its name means 'hairless' in Aztec.

Right: With its silky crest of hair on top of the head, and its hairless, softly dappled skin, the tiny Chinese Crested dog is a strange-looking but much prized and unusual rare breed.

Above: The Shar Pei, with its loose crumpled skin and broad drooping face, does look a bit like a solemn boxer and was, in fact, once a Chinese fighting dog. However, its temperament is quiet and friendly, which makes this a good, if bizarre-looking pet. A very rare breed.

Left: The sturdy Puli has an extraordinarily thick curly coat, which protects it from the extreme weather conditions of its native Hungarian plains. It is a loyal and obedient dog.

Below: The lionlike Chow Chow is famous for its unusual blue-black tongue, as well as its stocky body, thick woolly coat and curled spitzlike tail. It is a popular, successful show dog.

Right: It is the handsome wiry beard and moustache that makes the Griffin Bruxellois so distinctive and gives it a rather haughty, almost comical expression. It has a charming nature and makes a good small pet, although originally it was an efficient watch dog and rat catcher. The breed is rare outside Belgium and not easy to reproduce. Litters are small and delicate.

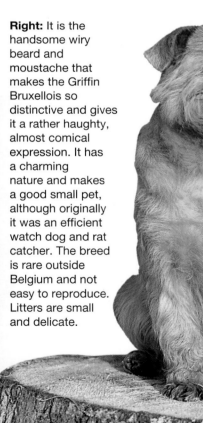

Below: The Komondor has a thick, curly fleecelike coat, suited to harsh conditions.

INDEX

Page numbers in **bold** indicate major references, including accompanying photographs. Page numbers in *italics* indicate captions to other illustrations. Less important text entries are shown in normal type.

PICTURE CREDITS

Photographers

The publishers wish to thank the following photographers and agencies who have supplied photographs for this book. The photographers have been credited by page number and position on the page: (B) Bottom, (T) Top, (C) Centre, (BL) Bottom Left, etc.

Marc Henrie: Title page, Copyright page (T), 8(BL), 8(CR), 9(TL), 11(BR), 12(BR), 13(TL), 13(TR), 13(BR), 15(CL), 16(BL), 17(TL), 18(T), 18(BR), 19(TL), 19(TR), 19(CR), 20-21(CB), 21(CR), 21(BR), 23(TL), 24(T), 24-25(CB), 25(TL), 25(TR), 25(BR), 26(BL), 26-27(CB), 27(CL), 27(BR), 28(T), 28(BL), 29(TL), 29(TR), 29(BR), 30(BL), 31(TR), 32(BL), 32-33(CB), 33(CT), 33(BR), 33(TR), 34(BL), 34-35(CB), 35(TL), 35(TR), 35(BR), 36(BL), 37(TL), 37(TR), 42(T), 43(TR), 43(BR), 53(T), 56(BL), 56(BR), 57(TR), 57(C), 59(BL)

Photo Researchers Inc.:

V.Andres/Okapia: 32(T)
Toni Angermayer: 53(CR), 55(BL), 57(BR), 58(BR)
H.G.Arndt/Okapia: 14(BR)
Bill Bachman: 41(BR)
Mike and Inge Bartlett/Okapia: 9(BL)
Charles R. Belinky: 15(TR)
Rolf Bender/Okapia: 30(T), 52(T)
Bildarchiv Okapia: 16(TR), 40(BL), 44(BL)
Gabrielle Boiselle/Okapia: 26(T)
Mary Eleanor Browning: Copyright page (B), 50-51(CB)
Alan Carey: 23(CL)
Porterfield-Chickering: 58(BL)
C.J.Collins: 31(CB)
Jerry Cooke: 22(BL), 24(BL), 37(BR), 54(T)
Kent and Donna Dannen: 47(BR), 47(TL), 49(CR), 57(BL)
Tim Davis: 19(BR)
John J. Dommers: 12(CL)
Francois Ducasse/Rapho: 41(TR)
James Foote: 21(C)
Lowell Georgia: 20(BL)
Dan Guravich: 46(BL)
Jan Halaska: 50(T)
Jack Hamilton: 23(TR)
Tom Hollyman: 12(BL)
C.D.Hotel/Jacana: 11(CL)
Ray Hunold: 17(BL)
Frederic/Jacana: 45(BL), 59(BR)

George E. Jones: 23(BR), 38(T)
J.M.Labat/Jacana: 7(TR)
M.Philip Kahl: 6-7(CB)
G.C.Kelly: 6(BL)
Stephen Krasemann: 48(T)
Susan Kuklin: 27(TR)
Elizabeth Lemoine/Okapia: 56(T), 57(TL)
Elizabeth Lemoine/Jacana: 17(BR)
Alexander Lowry: 31(CT)
Renee Lynn: 28-29(CB)
Hans-Jurgen Markmann/Okapia: 49(TL)
Susan McCartney: 47(TR)
Tom McHugh: 6(CT), 7(TL), 7(BR), 11(TL)
Carolyn A. McKeone: 31(BR), 45(BR), 46(T), 49(BR)
Bruno Meier/Okapia: 14(BL), 44(BR)
Mero/Jacana: 51(BR)
St.Meyers/Okapia: 49(BL)
Lawrence Migdale: 22(BR)
Peter Miller: 43(TL)
William H.Mullins: 22(T), 48(BL), 49(TR)
Robert Noonan: 41(TL)
Horst Pfingstagg/Okapia: 34(T), 44(T), 45(TL), 45(TR)
Louisa Preston: 13(CL), 55(CR)
Ann Purcell: 9(BR), 39(BL), 50(BL)
Hans Reinhard/Okapia: 9(TR), 11(TR), 15(TL), 15(CR), 15(CB), 18(BL), 30(BR), 38(BL), 46-47(CB), 52(BR), 53(BL), 55(BR), 58-59(CT)
Blair Seitz: 19(CB), 27(TL)
Gordon E. Smith: 21(TR), 48(BR)
Lee F. Snyder: 59(TR)
Jean-Paul Thomas/Jacana: 23(BL)
K.G.Vock/Okapia: 17(TR), 39(BR), 40(BR)
E.M.Vogeler/Okapia: 10(TR), 10(BL), 32(CB), 38-39(CB), 39(T), 40(T), 51(T), 53(BR), 55(TL), 59(CR)
Elisabeth Weiland: 20(T), 55(TR)
Jeanne White: 10-11(CB), 11(CR), 28(BR), 36-37(CB), 41(BL), 42(BL), 42-43(CB), 52(BL), 54(BL)
Ray Woolfe: 49(CL)
Ellan Young: 54(BR)